Ten Miracles of Jesus
WORKBOOK

Ten Miracles of Jesus
WORKBOOK

by Jamie Buckingham

Studies in the Gospels of Ten Miracles by Jesus Christ

To be used with "Ten Miracles of Jesus"
Video Tape Series

TEN MIRACLES OF JESUS
by
Jamie Buckingham

CONTENTS

Ten Miracles of Jesus

1. Miracles continue today.

2. God works His miracles through us.

3. The purpose of miracles is to glorify God.

4. True miracles always defy logic and understanding.

5. There is nothing as powerful as the name of Jesus in the mouth of a believer.

Ten Miracles of Jesus

INTRODUCTION

Read This First

There are two groups of people in the world. Those who believe all events have natural origin; and those who believe many events are supernatural in origin. For a number of years, since the famous Scopes trial in Tennessee, a great debate has raged in America concerning creation. Did this world come into being as a natural course of action, or was it formed by God—a supernatural event?

There is one group who believes this world evolved naturally—without the help of God. The other group believes God is active in the various processes of life—including creation. Those who believe that also believe in miracles.

Jesus belonged to the second group.

Not only did He believe God was active in all the processes of life—He proved it.

No problem, since Jesus was the son of God—endowed with all the power and authority which God, Himself, had.

That included the power to perform miracles.

A miracle is basically the involvement of God as He overrides (or works outside) the natural laws He has set in motion by superimposing his higher law for the moment—the law of love.

As we look at the miracles of Jesus we find they fall into several different categories.

There are healing miracles, such as the one He performed on the blind man at the Pool of Siloam.

There are miracles of creation, such as the miracle at Cana where He turned the water into wine, and the time He took five loaves and two small fish and multiplied them into enough food to feed the 5,000.

There are miracles of deliverance, where He took authority over evil spirits and cast them out—setting people free from what seemed to be madness and irrational behavior.

Then there are miracles over nature, such as the time He stood in the back of the boat and commanded a fierce storm to subside—or when He walked on water.

Miracles in the Bible—and miracles today—are always accompanied by fear and wonder. Why? Because they are exceptions to the known. They come from the unknown. They are more than natural. They are supernatural.

If you approach this subject by ruling out the supernatural you will see no miracles. You will be forced to say all such occurences have natural causes. If you are willing to admit God is a god of miracles—then you will begin to see them yourself. Such is the nature of faith—or belief.

Miracles reveal the nature of God. Thus there are no big miracles and little miracles. All miracles are big—for they reflect the nature of our big God. While they do, by definition, interrupt the usual course of nature, in so doing they assert all the more the unity and harmony of God for they reveal a God who not only created nature, but still controls it by the higher law of love. "The creation waits in eager expectation," Paul wrote, "for the sons of God to be revealed" (Romans 8:19). In short, all nature yearns for man to take his rightful place as a man of spiritual authority through whom miracles come as readily as they did though Jesus—the second Adam.

There is a great resurgence of interest in miracles—not only among Christians, but among all people. You can go into any bar in America, any pub in Europe, strike up a conversation about miracles, and you'll get a crowd. Especially if you're talking about one that happened to you. Folks will gather around. The followers of Jesus know that if they study Jesus' message, and trust in the Holy Spirit, they, too, can perform miracles.

On my last trip to Israel I took a camera crew with me. We visited the sites of ten of Jesus' best known miracles. There I video-taped a brief message concerning the event that happened at that place.

This workbook has been designed to be used with those taped video messages. The workbook will be best used in a small group of people who have a leader (teacher or instructor). Ideal usage calls for the same group to meet once a week for ten weeks. You'll need your Bible, because the questions in the workbook are all taken from the various scriptural accounts of Jesus' miracles. Each session should last about an hour and should begin as the group views the section of the video tape pretaining to the chapter to be studied. Each video segment runs about 10 minutes. Then the teacher, using this workbook as a guide, will lead the class in a study of the material at hand.

When this material was first produced some people complained that the video teaching segments were not long enough. However, I believe that while video is an important teaching tool (you could never see what I saw without it), it is not a substitute for the personalization brought by a teacher, a workbook, and a Bible.

What I have given you is the best of both methods.

Several years ago I produced a similar set of video tapes and a workbook called *The Journey to Spiritual Maturity*. In it I traced the footsteps of Moses through the Sinai, pausing to teach along the way. Shortly after that material was distributed I began getting letters from prison and jail chaplains—as well as Bible study leaders who were working with men and women behind bars. They were saying the material was ideal for prison Bible studies since it combined the visual (video) with the written (workbook) with an instructor. Video alone is not sufficient to convey truth. It must be combined with the personal touch of a teacher to answer—and ask—questions, and a workbook to stimulate actual Bible reading and study.

Encouraged that prisoners were using the material, I prepared three more series using the same technique. One series covered *Ten Parables of Jesus*. Another was called *Ten Bible People Like Me* and was a study of ten Bible heros. This one looks at *Ten Miracles of Jesus*. All were designed—from my teaching on location in Israel to the workbooks—to be used in prisons and jails where hundreds of thousands of men and women are eagerly learning more about God.

However, it soon became evident that what is good for prisoners, is good for all. Thus the material was slightly modified so it can be used just as easily by a Sunday school class or a home group as by a prison Bible study group.

As you study the miracles of Jesus, may you find the process of miracles at work in your own life. Miracles should be the norm in the life of the Christian. Because we are constantly stumbling through a dark world, we need God to guide our footsteps, giving us the ability to walk supernaturally. The purpose of this workbook is to stimulate you, excite you, hopefully to convince you that the miracles of Jesus were not just for yesterday—they are for today. They were not for Jesus alone, they are for you. It is not enough to say, "Expect a Miracle." You should say, "Expect a Miracle Through Me."

God is not restoring miracles to the body. The miracles have been there all along. He is simply waiting for simple people—in prison and out—who will step forward in faith and expect God to use them, as he used Jesus, to perform miracles.

Jamie Buckingham
Melbourne, Florida

GETTING THE MOST FROM THIS STUDY

Using the accompanying video tapes, this workbook is designed to lead you, step by step, into an understanding of the nature of miracles. In particular you will be studying ten of the miracles of Jesus. The video segments of these lessons were filmed on the locations in Israel where the miracles actually occurred. You will see the Sea of Galilee, the pools of Siloam and Bethesda, and the place where the swine, filled with demons, raced off the cliff into the sea. You will be as much a part of the audience as the group of people who accompanied the camera crew when the tapes were made.

Those miracles of Jesus—as wonderful and awesome as they were—are still being performed by people in whom the Risen Jesus lives. It is my prayer that as you study these events in your Bible and answer the questions in this workbook, you, too, will begin to exprience the miracles of Jesus—in your own life and ministry.

The material on the video tape and in this workbook can be used in a number of different ways. It can be the basis of an individual study. It may be used in a small group, such as a Bible study group, a Sunday school class, or a house group. Experience has shown the greatest benefit will come when a group of people study the material together under a leader who is well-prepared on the subject.

Helps for the Leader

If you are a leader preparing to take a group of people into a study on the miracles of Jesus, you should consider the following:

1. Necessary Materials

* A good color television set with a screen large enough to be seen by all present.

* A reliable video player

* A power source within reach of the plugs for the TV and VCR.

* Comfortable seating so each person may see the TV screen and the teacher.

* A Bible for each student. The workbook uses scripture quotes from the New International Version (NIV), but any Bible will do.

* A workbook for each student.

* Pen or pencil for each student.

Although parallel reading is not mandatory, it is helpful. I have written a book titled *The Miracles of Jesus—Then and Now*—which is designed to be used with this course. Published by Paraclete Press, Orleans, Massachusetts, it is a basic Bible commentary on the same miracles covered in this study, illustrated with modern day miracles of similar nature to the ones performed by Jesus. The book covers, in much greater detail, all the material presented in this course, as well as a wealth of other background information.

2. Preparation

Before teaching others you should not only view the entire video series—all 10 segments—but you should work your way through this workbook. You will find a number of scripture references. Study them in depth before attempting to lead the class in discussion. You are not expected to have all the answers. Your job will be to help the students ask the right questions and stimulate them to explore the Bible for themselves.

3. Be Aware

As you lead the class be aware that each person present is going through some kind of crisis in his or her life which can only be handled by a miracle. This could be a financial crisis, a grief experience, a problem with personal identification, a battle with demons or temptation, a crisis in the home, spiritual confusion, or a number of different mountains which seem too high to climb and too thick to tunnel through. Your awareness of their need for a miracle will help when it comes to answering questions and leading discussion. Do not be afraid to pause, at any place in the discussion, and minister to that person or persons—asking the class to join in expecting a miracle.

4. Stick to the Subject

Your job, as teacher, is to hold the discussion to miracles. There will always be those in the class who will want to lead you on some rabbit chase down a side path, will want to monopolize the discussion, or try to entice you into an argument over some minor point. It is important you stick, as nearly as possible, to the outline of the subject at hand. The material has been carefully designed to build principle on principle with the eventual aim of the student becoming "thoroughly equipped for every good work" (II Timothy 3:17). Do not preach. Do not monopolize the conversation yourself. Do not allow the class to drift from the subject matter.

5. Stimulate Discussion

Remember, your job as teacher is not to give answers—even if you know them—but to skillfully stimulate discussion and encourage each student to find God's Word for his own life. The Holy Spirit will help you, for He not only wants each student to know about the miracles of Jesus, He wants each one to experience the miracles—and to perform them himself. Do not limit yourself to the material covered in this workbook. It is merely a guide, a primer for discussion. Allow the Holy Spirit to direct your class sessions.

6. Be Sensitive to Time

If your class has more than an hour for each study, arrange for a break of a few minutes for refreshment or a stretch. If the group discussion is dynamic, or if someone in the class indicates a need for personal ministry, you may want to keep the session going. Or, if the particular subject is stimulating extra discussion, you may want to put off the next segment in order to continue that one for an additional week. If that is the case, I recommend the class review the same video segment at the opening of the second week of study to stimulate discussion.

Remember, just because the class has ended does not mean the Holy Spirit will not continue to work. In fact, in all probability the greatest work of the Spirit in the lives of the students will take place after the class is over. That means you may want to open the next class with a brief report on the Spirit's activity in the area of miracles since the class last met.

Helps for Students

Before you start this course ask yourself these questions:

* Am I really committed to finding God's will for my life?

* Am I willing to commit myself to attending all the sessions of this course unless unavoidably detained?

* Am I willing to open my mind to new truth beyond what I now believe?

* Am I willing to prepare ahead of time through prayer and by reading my Bible and doing work in my workbook?

* Am I willing to enter into the group discussion—asking questions and expressing my personal opinions?

* Am I willing, if I know God is prodding me, to ask for personal ministry that I might receive my own miracle?

* Am I willing, if someone else expresses a need, to be used by God that He might perform a miracle through me for the other person?

If you answered "no" to any of these questions you may want to reconsider whether you should take this course. You are getting ready to touch the Word of God, and to examine the heart of God's supernatural nature. You should not enter into this course lightly or unadvisedly. Once you begin a serious study of the miracles of Jesus, God, in all likelihood, will begin to do miraculous things to and through you. If you are not ready for that to happen, you may want to sit this one out.

On the other hand, if you answered "yes" to the questions you are ready to proceed. Following are some immediate steps you can take to insure maximum benefit from the course.

1. Set Goals

This course is designed to help you understand not only the miracles of Jesus, but the nature of God. It does not matter whether you are young or old, a seasoned Christian or just a seeker. God does not limit His miracles. Like the rain, which falls on the just and the unjust, God loves to give miracles to all who reach out to Him. The principles learned over these next several class sessions will help you first of all understand the miracles of Jesus, but more important, begin to experience them. Look ahead to what you need— and what kind of person you want to be. Do you need a miracle? What kind? Set a goal and let this study help you get there.

2. Honestly Evaluate Your Present Condition

What are your needs—your real needs? A prisoner may feel his primary need is to experience the kind of miracle Peter experienced when an angel came and opened the prison doors so he could walk free. On the other hand, remember Paul, too, was in prison in Philippi when an earthquake threw open the doors and loosed him from his shackles. Yet God told him to hang around, for the jailer would soon appear asking, "What must I do to be saved?" Your "evident" need may not be your need at all.

A woman approached me asking me to pray she would be healed of a painful back condition. However, as I layed hands on her and started to pray the Holy Spirit gave me insight that her need was not for healing of the muscle spasms in her back—but for a broken relationship with her daughter. Before I prayed, I asked her: "Tell me about your daughter?" She was shocked that I should focus in on that nagging, twisting, painful situation. She broke and began to cry, admitting she had thrown the daughter out of the house after the girl had insisted on getting an abortion. While the abortion, itself, was evil, her cruel, judgmental reaction to her daughter was equally sinful. The spiritual forces involved were literally twisting her back. When she forgave her daughter—her back was healed.

Honestly evaluate your present condition as you begin this study of miracles, for without a willingness to face yourself it will be extremely difficult to understand what God is saying to you concerning your past, present, and future.

The commitment to dig into the Bible and examine the miracle nature of God must be accompanied by constant self-measurement and self-inventory. You know the kind of person you already are. You know the level of commitment you already display. You know your faith level. The question you must now face is not "Can I conjure up enough faith to experience a miracle?" but, "Am I willing to place myself in a position where God can work His miracles in and through me?"

At the end of each chapter there is a place where you—in the privacy of your own study—can evaluate your personal progress. The answers you give to the questions will give you a spiritual indicator of your progress week by week. The questions will also help fix the Word of God more firmly in your heart, and thus provide a reservoir of truth that the Holy Spirit can draw upon in the training and reshaping of your life until you are conformed to the image of Jesus.

3. You'll Not Pass This Way Again

Although God gives each man and woman infinite chances to improve and move into spiritual maturity, there are certain times when miracles are offered—and if refused—are not offered again. Thus, when discussion in class opens the door for you to express yourself, or ask for prayer for a miracle, do not hesitate to respond. One of the things you will be doing during these sessions will be learning to hear God—just as Jesus did.

When Jesus was urged to hasten to Jerusalem to heal His friend, Lazarus, He waited. He knew God had a bigger miracle in store than healing His sick friend. God was planning on a resurrection.

On the other hand, when blind Bartimaeus, sitting beside a dusty road in old Jericho, heard Jesus was passing by, he cried out in a loud voice, begging Jesus to have mercy on him. Jesus, hearing the blind begger calling His name, responded immediately. Would Jesus have healed the man had he not asked? No one knows. What we do know is that the man asked—and Jesus responded immediately.

In both cases—the case of Lazarus and the case of Bartimaeus—Jesus heard God before acting. Earlier He had said, "I do only what the Father tells me to do."

I urge you, therefore, to hear God—and do what He tells you to do, regardless of how illogical it may seem at the time. Only those who seek help find it. Only those who are open to receive a miracle, receive it.

4. Study Each Chapter Before Class

Ideally, you should study each chapter in this workbook *before* coming to class. Look up each Scripture reference, answer all the questions by filling in the blanks and circling the true/false answers. Of course, if it is impossible to study ahead of time, you should still take part in the class activities.

5. Set Your Own Pace

One of the lessons you will learn as you study the Bible is this: God's patience is infinite as long as you are moving toward Him. The only time you will begin to feel pressure is when you close your mind, dig in your heels, or get off God's trail by pursuing false ideas and concepts. Do not be afraid to move slowly. To rush through this study may mean you learn all the right religious answers, but miss the Holy Spirit, who is the one who brings miracles today. This course is designed to provoke you to do your own searching, thinking, and praying—that you may see concrete results from your faith in God.

6. Check Your Progress

Once you have completed the course, ask your chaplain, pastor, or group leader to sit down with you and review where you are in life. Remember the question Jesus asked the man at the pool of Bethesda: "Do you really want to be healed?" A lot of people want to see miracles, but are not sure they want to experience one themselves.

7. Finally

Unless otherwise stated Scripture quotations are taken from the New International Version (NIV) of the Bible, copyright 1978 by New York International Bible Society and published by Zondervan Corporation, Grand Rapids, Michigan. Used by permission. Each chapter has a number of questions with accompanying Scripture references. By looking up the references you should be able to answer all the questions. Do not be afraid to fill in the blanks— even if you give the wrong answer. No one is going to grade you. This course is like those wonderful Special Olympics for handicapped children—everyone who enters is called a winner, regardless of how he finishes.

You will be awarded a Certificate of Completion at the end of the course, signed by me and your instructor. All you have to do is finish. That makes you a winner. By looking up the answers you will learn. Go ahead, try it. It's fun to learn—especially when you are learning about God.

And remember, the only thing more exciting than receiving a miracle, is letting God work through you to perform one.

Jamie Buckingham

Lesson 1
The Wedding Feast
He Turned the Water into Wine

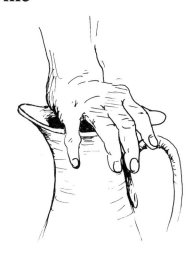

SCRIPTURE: John 2:1-11
VIDEO REFERENCE: Lesson #1
SUPPLEMENTARY READING REFERENCE:
 The Miracles of Jesus: Then—and Now
 Chapter I: "Nothing But the Best"

The miracles of Jesus fall into five general categories:

 (1) *Miracles of healing.* These include giving sight to the blind, healing cripples, and curing diseases such as leprosy.

 (2) *Miracles over nature.* These miracles include such instances as walking on water and stilling the Galilean storm.

 (3) *Miracles of deliverance.* Stories abound of Jesus setting people free from evil spirits. Some of these people had been made sick by the demons, but when Jesus commanded the demons to leave they were healed as well.

 (4) *Miracles of resurrection.* On several occasions Jesus spoke life back into dead bodies. Indeed, he experienced such a miracle himself near the close of his earthly ministry.

 (5) *Miracles of creation.* In these miracles Jesus brought things into being which had not been there before. On one occasion food was provided for 5,000 people on a hillside. On another occasion water was turned into wine.

It was this miracle, a miracle of creation—which was the first recorded act of His Father who created the entire earth—that Jesus performed to begin his public ministry.

BIBLE STUDY

1. The Purpose of Miracles.

The purpose for all miracles is to glorify God. Miracles have no other purpose. All miracles come from God and are designed to give God the glory and the credit. God does not want man to get the credit or the glory. God will not share His glory with any other.

What does God say about sharing His glory? (Isaiah 48:11)

_____

2. **Power for Working Miracles**

At the time Jesus was baptized in the Jordan River by John the Baptist, the Holy Spirit came upon Him, giving Him the power to perform miracles.

Are there any recorded miracles of Jesus prior to the miracle at Cana which occured after His baptism in water? (John 2:11)

_____ Yes

_____ No

How did John and the others at the Jordan River know the Holy Spirit had come upon Jesus? (Matthew 3:16)

_____

_____

_____

Is Jesus the only one who needed to be baptized in the Holy Spirit? (Acts 1:5)

_____ Yes

_____ No

At Pentecost the followers of Jesus were all baptized in the Holy Spirit.

Besides the 120, who else did Peter say should receive the gift of the Holy Spirit? (Acts 2:39)

_____

_____

_____

Where did Jesus say we were to be witnesses of Him? (Acts 1:8)

(1)_____

(2)_____

(3)_____

(4)_____

How do these areas of the earth correspond with the place where you live? **List what you feel are the four corresponding areas of the earth compared to where you are now living—the places where you should be witnessing.**

(1) Jerusalem = _____

(2) Judea = _____

(3) Samaria = _____

(4) The Uttermost part of the earth = _____

_____

What happened to Jesus following his baptism in water? (Luke 4:1)

_____

_____

_____

Following his temptation in the wilderness, Jesus returned to Galilee to begin His public ministry.

By comparing Luke 4:1 with Luke 4:14, tell what was different about Jesus.

_____

_____

_____

3. **The Setting for the First Miracle**

Jesus first miracle was at a small, terraced community on a steep mountainside near his home town of Nazareth—just a few miles west and south of the Sea of Galilee.

What was the name of the village where all this happened? (John 2:1)

_____

Who was the hostess at the wedding reception? (John 2:1-5)

_____

It was a typical village wedding feast. Jewish law called for the wedding of a virgin to begin on Wednesday. But, like all weddings, this one lasted more than one day. The wedding ceremony itself took place late in the evening after a feast. After dinner the young couple would be escorted through the village streets to their new home with the light of flaming torches and a canopy over their heads.

During this happy time Jesus and his disciples attended the festivities. Jesus had just met these "disciples" three days before. At that time He had only called four men to follow him. They were strangers to the people in town, but because of the respect the villagers had for Jesus, they welcomed His friends also.

List the names of the four disciples who accompanied Jesus to the wedding. (John 1:40-51)

(1)_____

(2)_____

(3)_____

(4)_____

What problem presented itself at the wedding? (John 2:3)

_____

_____

4. About Wine

For a Jewish feast wine was essential. "Without wine," the ancient rabbis said, "there is no joy." As usual, fresh wine was served at the weddings—not the kind that that had been kept around and aged for a long time.

Drunkeness, however, was forbidden. The scriptures commanded against it.

There are four kinds of wine mentioned in the Bible.

(1) *Oxos*, a type of vinegar (Matthew 27:48; Mark 15:36)

(2) *Gleuchos*, a sweet "new" wine, a stronger drink (Acts 2:13)

(3) *Sikera*, an intoxicating grain wine (Luke 1:15)

(4) *Oinos*, a pure grape wine, only slightly alcoholic (Luke 22:18)

The wine served at Jewish weddings was customarily *oinos*. (This was the kind of wine used at the wedding at Cana, and the kind of wine Jesus later created.) Since it was drunk in great quantities, it was usually mixed with water—normally two parts water to one part wine—to prevent drunkenness.

This was a common practice, not only at weddings, but at the Passover as well where the Gemara—one of the Jewish documentary guides—commanded: "The cup of blessing is not to be blessed until it is mixed with water."

Wine is the only alcoholic drink mentioned in the Bible. (The process of distilling beverages to produce "hard liquor" was unknown until the 13th century.) Wine was the common drink of the New Testament.

What does the Bible have to say about drinking strong drink? (Proverbs 23:31)

_____

_____

Name the results of drinking strong drink. (Proverbs 23:29)

(1)_____

(2)_____

(3)_____

(4)_____

(5)_____

(6)_____

Why did Paul tell Timothy to "drink a little wine?" (I Timothy 5:23)

_____

5. **The Miracle**

What did Jesus' mother, who was hostess at the wedding, tell the servants? (John 2:5)

_____

_____

How many water jars were nearby? (John 2:6)

_____

What were they normally used for? (John 2:6)

_____

What was normally washed in ceremonial washings? (Mark 7:3-4)

_____

_____

How much did each jar hold? (John 2:6)

_____

Besides Jesus and His mother, who else knew the water had been turned into wine? (John 2:7-9)

_____

Exactly when and where was the water turned into wine? (John 2:7-9)

Check correct answer:

_____ (1) In the urns.

_____ (2) When dipped from the urns into the smaller container.

_____ (3) When it was poured into the cup.

_____ (4) When the banquet master tasted it.

_____ (5) The Bible does not say.

6. **The purpose of the miracle**

   What were the two results of this miracle? (John 2:11)

   (1)_____

   (2)_____

WRAP UP

It is meaningful that Jesus chose an ordinary ceremony—a wedding—to perform his first miracle. God always uses the ordinary. When the angel came to Mary to tell her she had conceived, He met her—not in the Temple—but in a private place. When it was time for the Son of God to be born, He was birthed in a stable. It was shepherds who received the first angelic visit. The Son of God spent His early years in a carpenter's shop. God is a god of the ordinary. How appropriate that the first miracle would be at the wedding of a nameless village peasant who was suffering the embarrassment of having run out of wine.

Jesus wanted us to know that not only does God enjoy celebrations—He is a God of the ordinary. Miracles are not reserved for heads of state, missionaries and television preachers—they are for us. They take place in impossible situations—when the wine runs out—to teach us man's extremity is God's opportunity, and that delays of mercy are not to be construed as denials of prayer.

FINAL LESSONS

Miracles reveal the nature of God.

Not only is God a joyful God, He wants us filled with joy, too.

PERSONAL REVIEW QUESTIONS

Circle T (true) or F (false)

1. T   F   Jesus' first miracle took place in His home.

2. T   F   Everybody in Nazareth knew Jesus was the Son of God.

3. T   F   Jesus turned water into wine to let us know it's okay to get drunk every once in a while.

4. T   F   Miracles are for everyone, not just Christians.

5. T   F   There are four kinds of alcoholic drinks mentioned in the Bible, but only one kind of wine.

6. T   F   Mary commanded Jesus to turn the water into wine.

7. T   F   The wine made by God was better than the wine made by man.

8. T   F   Miracles are reserved for preachers, missionaries, and television evangelists.

9. T   F   No one knows exactly where and when the actual miracle—the water turning into wine—took place.

10. T   F   Jesus turned water into wine to reveal His glory.

MEMORY VERSE

John 2:11 (Memorize, then write it on these lines.)

_____

_____

_____

TRUE OR FALSE ANSWERS:

1-F, 2-F, 3-F, 4-T, 5-F, 6-F, 7-T, 8-F, 9-T, 10-T

NOTES

Lesson 2
Jesus Stills A Storm
Power Over Nature

SCRIPTURE: Mark 4:35-41
         (also Matthew 8:23-27 and Luke 8:22-25)
VIDEO REFERENCE: Lesson #2
SUPPLEMENTARY READING REFERENCE:
    The Miracles of Jesus: Then—and Now
    Chapter II: "Power Over Nature"

Nothing frustrates people more than our inability to take authority over inanimate objects. People take great satisfaction in training animals, in discovering new ways to combat disease, in solving mathematical and scientific problems. We feel fulfilled when faced with a problem—such as trying to figure out how to build a bridge across a river—and solve that problem using engineering, construction, economic and managerial skills. We have developed vaccines which have virtually wiped out diseases such as polio, smallpox, and bubonic plague. We have learned that it is possible to set and splint broken bones, meaning people don't have to have their bodies disfigured for life simply because they broke a leg as a child.

But there are certain things man hasn't been able to do anything about. The weather is one of them. We can barely predict it. We have weather forecasters and meteorologists and hurricane specialists. We send up weather balloons, fly airplanes into the center of hurricanes, and forecast weather patterns from satellites. But forecasting and reporting is all we can do. No one has yet figured out how to change, must less control, the weather. Even Jesus said the "wind blows wherever it pleases" (John 3:8). In short, we can predict the weather but we can't do anything about it.

Yet, as we read the Bible we find numbers of times where men, under the anointing of God, took authority over nature. Moses held out his rod over the waters of the Red Sea and they parted. Joshua, needing more daylight to finish his battle against the combined armies of the Amorites, commanded "the sun to stand still." But it's the story of Jesus' authority over the wind and waves that gives us the best insight into God's miracles over nature.

1. **The Fear Factor**

The Sea of Galilee is a large lake surrounded by high hills on three sides. Therefore it is subject to sudden squalls. The disciples, experienced fishermen, were used to such storms. Their high-sided boats were capable of staying afloat in almost any weather.

What time of day did this take place? (Mark 4:35)

_____ (1) Early morning

_____ (2) Noon

_____ (3) After dark

What did Matthew say was different about this storm? (Matthew 8:24)

_____

Where was Jesus when this storm blew up? (Mark 4:38)

_____ (1) Down in the hold of the ship

_____ (2) In the stern of the boat

_____ (3) Out walking on the water

What was Jesus doing? (Mark 4:38)

_____

What did the disciples do when faced with fear of circumstances beyond their control? (Matthew 8:25)

_____

2. **Faith Faces Danger**

There are basically two kinds of miracles. There are those miracles which happen because God Himself intervenes. No prayer, no faith, no human agent is involved. God simply overrides a law of nature because He sees what needs to take place and there is no man there to do it.

Other miracles involve man. In these man is the agent God uses to bring the miracles to pass. When man is involved faith becomes a major factor. What is faith? Faith is simply believing God is in charge and has given to man all the dominion He gave to Jesus.

When man is involved in miracles, faith becomes a major factor.

What is the Bible's classic definition of faith? (Hebrews 11:1)

_____

_____

_____

The Word of God is the basis for our faith. We believe because God has spoken, not because we see the results. When we believe because we see results that is called knowledge. When we believe on the basis of God's word, that is called faith.

What had Jesus said that should have been the basis of the disciples' faith? (Mark 4:35)

_____

_____

How much faith did the disciples have? (Matthew 8:26)

_____ (1) As much as a grain of mustard seed

_____ (2) Enough to remove mountains

_____ (3) Big faith

_____ (4) Little faith

What did Jesus say we could do if we have faith in Him? (John 14:12)

_____

_____

_____

3. The Dominion of Jesus

Faith is believing that God is, that He is good, and that He wants to work through you. Sin is rebellion against God and His plan, saying, "God is not who He says He is. I can't trust Him, I can't believe Him. I'm going to do things my way. "

Jesus came to earth to overcome sin. His presence re-establishes our belief in God. He brings us back to God. Atonement, which is what Jesus does, (he atones for our sin) is a bridge between man in his sin, and God in His holiness. Jesus is our atonement. He bridges that gap so we can understand who God is.

Through whom did sin enter the world? (Romans 5:12)

_____

What are the wages of sin? (Romans 6:23)

_____

Who does Paul say Adam was? (Romans 5:14)

_____

Sin started with Adam. It is sin that keeps us from believing. Lack of faith keeps us from receiving and performing miracles.

If death came from Adam, what does Jesus Christ bring? (I Corinthians 15:21)

_____

_____

Adam was a "pattern of one to come."

Who is the "last Adam?" (I Corinthians 15:45)

_____

Jesus came with all the dominion Adam had in the Garden of Eden. It was Jesus' dominion over all things—including nature—which gave Him the authority to stand up in the boat and say to nature, "I'm going to override you. I am in charge here. You, natural law, you, wind and waves, hear me! Your boss, your creator is speaking! I'm telling you to change, to stop this, to be calm, to sit down and to shut up."

God gave Jesus the same dominion He gave Adam in the Garden. Now Jesus has passed that along to all those who welcome Him as Lord.

4. God Gives Men Authority Over Nature

Man has dominion over the things of this world because Christ is in him. Jesus was, and is, the Living God. When He comes into us in the person of His Holy Spirit, He brings with him all His power and authority.

What is the hope of glory? (Colossians 1:27)

_____

What have we been given? (Colossians 2:10)

_____

What is Jesus head over? (Colossians 2:10)

(1)_____

(2)_____

Man has learned to scientifically predict weather though he cannot control it. But the Bible is full of stories of times when miracles happened to reverse "natural" processes.

What happened when Moses held his rod over the Red Sea? (Exodus 14:21-30)

_____

_____

When Joshua needed more hours of daylight to finish off Israel's enemies in battle, what did he do? (Joshua 10:12,13)

_____ (1) He commanded his axe head to float on the water

_____ (2) He held out his rod over the Red Sea

_____ (3) He commanded the sun to stand still

_____ (4) He climbed out of the boat and walked on water

_____ (5) He shouted and the walls of Jericho fell down

Nature is God's creation. Thus nature's unpredictable wildness can only be tamed by God. Jesus was, and is, the Living God. As His stewards of the earth, our responsibility includes rebuking Satan when he causes the weather to go on a destructive rampage.

How do we know we have the same kind of authority that Jesus has? (John 14:12)

_____

_____

_____

Jesus never performed a miracle for His own benefit. He never changed a camel into a Cadillac. His miracles were for one purpose only—for the glory of God. He never profited a single time.

What did Jesus tell Satan when tempted to change rocks into bread? (Luke 4:3-4)

_____

_____

_____

The idea that we have authority over the weather is foreign to us. But let's pause and consider: God did not set certain laws of the universe in motion, then step back out of the way. Rather, He has given us the same authority He gave Jesus to override these laws—when it is His will—so that His higher purpose may be accomplished.

In the incident on the Sea of Galilee, Satan used the weather to try to keep Jesus from "crossing over to the other side" as He said was His intention.

How is Satan described? (Ephesians 2:2)

_____

_____

Following the temptation experience Satan withdrew from Jesus, but he indicated he would return to try to destroy Him.

When was it said he would return to attack Jesus? (Luke 4:13)

_____

Satan chose this occasion, while Jesus was asleep in the boat, to try to murder Him.

Who does Jesus say Satan is? (John 8:44)

(1)_____

(2)_____

What question did the disciples ask after Jesus performed His miracle? (Mark 4:41)

_____

_____

_____

WRAP UP

Jesus overrode Satan's use of the laws of nature by evoking the higher law of love. He took dominion over the wind and waves and performed a miracle.

We have dominion over anything that interrupts the will and purpose of God in our lives, the will and purpose of God on earth.

FINAL LESSONS

We have dominion in Christ; but we must take dominion over this world.

PERSONAL REVIEW QUESTIONS

1. T   F   The power Jesus gives us is the power of the Holy Spirit.

2. T   F   The whole crowd that had been listening to Jesus preach went out in boats.

3. T   F   Jesus and His disciples were asleep when the storm blew up.

4. T   F   Jesus was tired, so He went to sleep because God had already told Him they would go to the other side of the Sea.

5. T   F   When they woke Him, Jesus told the disciples, "Quiet! Be still!"

6. T   F   Faith is simply believing God is in charge.

7. T   F   Faith copes with fear by recalling God's Word then calling on God's power to change the situation.

8. T   F   Man has dominion over the things of this world because Christ is in him.

9. T   F   After rebuking the storm Jesus rebuked his disciples for not believing they would arrive safely at the other side.

10. T   F   After He rebuked the storm Jesus got out of the boat and walked on the water to prove he was God.

11. T   F   Nature is subject to God's command, even though that command may be spoken through the lips of a man.

MEMORY VERSE

Mark 4:41 (Memorize, then write it on these lines)

_____

_____

_____

TRUE OR FALSE ANSWERS:
1-T, 2-F, 3-F, 4-T, 5-F, 6-T, 7-T, 8-T, 9-T, 10-F, 11-T

25

NOTES

Lesson 3
Set Free From Demons
Jesus Confronts a Maniac

SCRIPTURE: Mark 5:1-20
        (Also Matthew 8:28-34 and Luke 8:26-39)
VIDEO REFERENCE: Lesson #3
SUPPLEMENTARY READING REFERENCE:
    The Miracles of Jesus: Then—and Now
    Chapter III: "Power Over Many Demons"

BIBLE STUDY

1. The Source of Evil

Satan's most powerful tactic is to convince spiritual leaders that demons do not exist, allowing them to do their evil work without interference from the very ones God has appointed to combat them.

Paul states that we are not contending with people but with what kind of spiritual forces? (Ephesians 6:12)

_____

_____

Where do these "forces of evil" operate? (Ephesians 6:12)

_____

Isaiah describes how the archangel Lucifer—known in the New Testament as Satan—tried to assume full power over God.

List the things—the five "I wills"—Lucifer intended to do? (Isaiah 14:13-14)

  (1) I will _____

     _____

(2) I will _____

_____

(3) I will _____

_____

_____

(4) I will _____

_____

(5) I will _____

_____

When God removed Lucifer from Heaven, where did He send him? (Isaiah 14:12)

_____

Who else was hurled there besides Satan? (Revelation 12:7-9)

_____

Lucifer, then, was not the only one banished from heaven. Expelled with him was his vast retinue of angels, plus the countless number of "little angels." They make up the demon force of Satan. Since they have no form, they are forced to take up habitation in living beings. Demons sometimes possess animals, but are usually assigned to humans.

What did Jesus say would eventually happen to the devil and his evil angels? (Revelation 20:10)

_____

_____

The Jews of Jesus' day believed the Decapolis—the area where Jesus delivered the man possessed by a legion of demons—was the geographical headquarters of Satan and his demons. This, then, was an area which had been turned over to Satan by its inhabitants. In Genesis 18:16 to 19:29, Abraham pleaded with God to spare the evil cities of Sodom and Gomorrah, where his nephew Lot lived.

Why was God unable to spare these places? (Genesis 18:20)

_____

_____

_____

Many years after Abraham the prophet, Daniel, exiled in Babylon, fasted and prayed for three weeks for deliverance of the Jews from the Babylonians. His prayers were not answered until an angel visited him with an explanation.

Who resisted the angel's coming in response to Daniel's prayers? (Daniel 10:13)

_____

What was the name of the archangel who came to fight the demonic ruler of that area? (Daniel 10:13)

_____

2. God's Authority in Spiritual Warfare

In studying this particular event which took place early in the public ministry of Jesus, we need to keep in mind something He said at the close of His public ministry—actually His final recorded words before ascending to heaven. At that time He said "All authority in heaven and on earth has been given to me. Therefore go and make disciples of all nations, baptizing them in the name of the Father and of the Son and of the Holy Spirit, and teaching them to obey everything I have commanded you. And surely I will be with you always, to the very end of the age" (Matthew 28:18-20).

How much authority had God actually given to Jesus? (Matthew 28:18)

_____

_____

Several years after the resurrection, the apostle Paul traveled to Athens, Greece, to share the gospel. Standing on Mars Hill, he preached a deeply intellectual sermon on "The Unknown God." The people were impressed, but no one became a disciple. Discouraged, Paul left Athens and traveled to Corinth. During his journey God convinced him he was taking the wrong approach to evangelism. When he reached Corinth he corrected his mistake.

Paul told the Corinthians he had changed his method of preaching. No longer would he try to impress them as he had tried in Athens.

What two things had Paul determined to leave out of his sermons? (I Corinthians 2:1)

(1)_____

(2)_____

What was the one thing Paul said he wanted to share with the Corinthians? (I Corinthians 2:2)

_____

_____

Name three things that Paul said he experienced when he preached about Jesus? (I Corinthians 2:3)

(1)_____

(2)_____

(3)_____

What was Paul determined to show the Corinthians? (I Corinthians 2:4)

_____

Paul had learned that the purpose of miracles was to demonstrate the power of God so others might see, have faith in God, and become disciples.

Paul tells us we have the armor of God which gives us power to stand against the devil and his demons.

List the six pieces of armor. (Ephesians 6:13-17)

(1)_____

(2)_____

(3)_____

(4)_____

(5)_____

(6)_____

3. Dealing With Identity

In the story at hand we find that as Jesus and His disciples carefully made their way through the graveyard at Gadara, a wild man—naked, screaming, hair flying, broken chains hanging from his wrists and ankles—leapt out toward them. There is a distinct contrast here between the man and the demons, shown by their response to Jesus.

When the man saw Jesus how did he respond? (Mark 5:6)

_____

_____

What did the demons then do? (Mark 5:7)

_____

_____

Yet the demons, themselves, were forced to recognize Jesus for who He was. They called him _Elion,_ "Most High God"—the term reserved for Jehovah alone. If you need any kind of proof that Jesus is the Messiah, ask a demon.

How do demons react to God? (James 2:19)

_____

Why did the man live in the tombs? (Luke 8:29)

_____

When Jesus asked the demons to identify themselves, the chief demon spoke out of the man, using the man's voice.

What name did the demon give? (Mark 5:9)

_____

4. **Dealing With Health**

It's possible the man Jesus encountered in the graveyard was afraid of wholeness. Part of him—his soul—was rushing toward Jesus; the other part—his mind—was backing off. It's the perennial struggle with God.

What was the man's greatest fear? (Luke 8:28)

_____

What was the demons' greatest fear? (Luke 8:31)

_____

Jews would not have been raising pigs because of their kosher laws, but they were raised in the Greek communities of Decapolis. The pigs couldn't handle the demons any better than the man had, and rushed off the cliff to be drowned.

How did the townspeople react? (Mark 5:15,17)

_____

_____

There is a price that goes with the presence of Jesus Christ.

What did Jesus say we must give up if we are to follow Him? (Luke 14:33)

_____

How was the man dressed when Jesus first saw him? (Luke 8:27)

_____

What did he do after he was delivered from demons? (Mark 5:15)

_____

What did the man want to do after he was made whole? (Mark 5:18)

_____

_____

What did Jesus tell him to do instead? (Mark 5:19)

_____

_____

What was the effect of his healing on the people of the area? (Mark 5:20)

_____

WRAP UP

The man, naturally, wanted to go with Jesus. He wanted to become one of His disciples. Jesus had another plan, however. The man was to become a witness for Jesus Christ. Earlier, Jesus had told some of His disciples if they would lay down their fishermen's nets and follow Him, He would make them fishers of men. With this man, however, Jesus broke the pattern. Instead of being a disciple, Jesus wanted him to be a witness. He was to be a living, walking, unquestionable demonstration of the miracle power of Jesus Christ.

FINAL LESSON

While all of us are not called to follow Jesus in full time ministry, we are all called to be witnesses to the people around us.

PERSONAL REVIEW QUESTIONS

Circle T (true) or F (false)

1. T   F   Since Jesus was God He never questioned whether He had authority over demons.

2. T   F   Evangelism is not only telling people about Jesus, it is also demonstrating Jesus' power and authority so others might see, have faith in God, and become disciples.

3. T   F   One of Satan's most powerful tactics is to convince spiritual leaders that demons do not exist.

4. T   F   God loves to force us against our will.

5. T   F   The man cut himself with rocks because he was so upset that the people of the area were eating ham.

6. T   F   The demons were eager to go into the pigs because they loved ham.

7. T   F   There is a price that goes with the presence of Christ in our lives.

8. T   F   The people were very happy to see the man delivered from demons.

9. T   F   The man, now free, wanted to go with Jesus.

10. T   F   Jesus told the man to get dressed and follow Him as one of His disciples.

MEMORY VERSE

Ephesians 6:12 (Memorize, then write it on these lines.)

_____

_____

_____

TRUE OR FALSE ANSWERS:

1-T, 2-T, 3-T, 4-F, 5-F, 6-F, 7-T, 8-F, 9-T, 10-F

NOTES

Lesson 4
Loaves and Fishes
Jesus Feeds 5,000 People

SCRIPTURE: John 6:1-15
　　　　　　(Also Matthew 14:13-21; Mark 6:30-44; Luke 9:10-17)
VIDEO REFERENCE: Lesson 4
SUPPLEMENTARY READING REFERENCE:
　　The Miracles of Jesus: Then—and Now
　　Chapter VIII: "Enough for Everyone"

BIBLE STUDY

1. The Passover Feast

It was the time of the Passover Feast. Great crowds of pilgrims from the north were moving south through the nation of Israel toward Jerusalem. Most were walking. A few were riding donkeys. The pilgrimage took about three weeks—a week to travel, another week to celebrate the feast in Jerusalem, and a final week to return. Many Galilean pilgrims traveling to Jerusalem crossed the Jordan River at the fords near the village of Bethsaida Julias, just north of the Sea of Galilee. Skirting the lake on the east side, they traveled south through the region of Peraea, re-crossing the Jordan near Jericho. The route was longer but it avoided the territory of the hated and dangerous Samaritans who lived along the west bank of the Jordan and west to a line that extended from Nazareth almost to Jerusalem.

What event in Jewish history does the Passover Feast commemorate?
(Exodus 12:21-23)

_____

_____

What were fathers supposed to tell their children when they asked what the Passover feast meant ? (Exodus 12:26-27)

_____

_____

_____

The Passover held special significance for Jesus, since it spoke of a hope for future deliverance which involved Him.

When John the Baptist identified Jesus with the Passover, what did he call Him? (John 1:29)

_____

What did the apostle Paul call Jesus? (I Corinthians 5:7)

_____

2. **The Setting of the Miracle**

   What significant event had taken place just prior to this miracle? (Matthew 14:1-11)

   _____

   _____

   How had Jesus found out about this? (Matthew 14:12)

   _____

   What did Jesus do when He heard the news? (Matthew 14:13)

   _____

   _____

   Did the crowds respect his need for a quiet time by himself? (Matthew 14:13)

   _____ Yes

   _____ No

Jesus had been teaching in Capernaum, and when he finished it was late afternoon. He and His disciples got in a couple of fishing boats and set sail around the coast about four miles to the little town of Bethsaida—hoping to be alone. But the people had been watching with astonishment the things Jesus had been doing, and rushed along the shore line to the place where the Jordan River flows into the lake from the north. Expecting Jesus to head for the fords of the Jordan at Bethsaida Julius, they raced toward the little village—many of them actually arriving before Jesus did.

What was Jesus reaction to these clamoring, selfish people? (Matthew 14:14)

_____ (1) He shook the dust from His sandals

_____ (2) He called them a generation of vipers

_____ (3) He called them whited sepulchres filled with dead men's bones

_____ (4) He had compassion on them.

Just a few days earlier Jesus had commissioned His disciples and sent them out to do miracles.

What power and authority had He given them? (Luke 9:1)

(1) _____

(2) _____

Jesus had told them to take no provision for their journey. He specifically told them to leave five things behind as they traveled.

What things were not allowed on the trip? (Luke 9:3)

(1) _____

(2) _____

(3) _____

(4) _____

(5) _____

Were the disciples successful in their miracle ministry? (Luke 9:6)

_____ Yes

_____ No

Why did the crowd, who were on their way to Jerusalem for the Passover Feast, turn aside and follow Jesus? (John 6:2)

_____

How did Jesus describe the crowd? (Mark 6:34)

_____

3. **Jesus Provides a Feast**

Seeing the huge crowd, which numbered 5,000 men alone (not to mention the women and children which could have swelled the mob to as many as 15,000), the disciples were worried.

What did the disciples ask Jesus to do? (Luke 9:12)

_____

_____

Jesus then did an astonishing thing.

What did He order His disciples to do? (Luke 9:13)

_____

Then turning to Philip, Jesus asked a question.

What did Jesus ask Philip? (John 6:5)

_____

_____

The nearest town was the villge of Bethsaida.

Which of the disciples were from Bethsaida? (John 1:44)

(1)_____

(2)_____

(3)_____

Who was the other disciple to get involved in the conversation? (John 6:8)

_____

Who did Andrew bring to Jesus? (John 6:9)

_____

_____

_____

Andrew had great faith that Jesus would multiply the loaves and fishes. (John 6:9)

_____ True

_____ False

What did Jesus want the crowd to do? (John 6:10)

_____ (1) Divide themselves into small groups and pray

_____ (2) Repent of their sins

_____ (3) Give money so Philip could go into town and buy food

_____ (4) Sit down on the grass

How much did each person receive? (John 6:11)

_____

How much was left over? (John 6:13)

_____

Why do you think there were 12 baskets used to collect the surplus? (John 6:13-14)

_____ (1) Because 12 is the perfect number in the Bible

_____ (2) Since there are 12 months in the year, this was a symbol that God provides for us all year long.

_____ (3) Because there were 12 tribes in the land of Israel

_____ (4) This is a reference to Leviticus 24:5 where God commanded Moses to bake 12 loaves of bread to be placed on the table in the Tabernacle.

_____ (5) Because Heaven has 12 gates made of pearl

_____ (6) Because there were 12 disciples and each one had a basket

When does the Bible say the miracle of multiplication actually took place? (John 6:10-14)

_____ (1) When Jesus blessed the loaves and fishes

_____ (2) When He handed them to the disciples

_____ (3) When the disciples began to distribute them

_____ (4) As the people reached into the baskets

_____ (5) No one knows

Seeing His ability to provide food, what did the people want to do with Jesus? (John 6:15)

_____

What was Jesus' response to this? (John 6:15)

_____

Later, the crowd caught up with Jesus once again, following Him to the other side of the lake. There He talked to them about their need for spiritual food as well as physical food.

What did Jesus call Himself? (John 6:35)

_____

There are several major characters in this story.

Aside from Jesus, who do you think is the real hero of the story?

_____ (1) Philip, who asked the hard questions

_____ (2) Andrew, who brought a little boy to Jesus

_____ (3) The little boy, who offered his lunch to meet the need

WRAP UP

Men are constantly looking at needs and saying there is no way to fill them; looking at situations and saying they are impossible. God is waiting for someone with faith the size of a mustard seed to step forward and offer what he has. God then multiplies the little and makes it great.

FINAL LESSON

All that is required for a miracle is someone who is willing to listen, obey, and get out of the way.

PERSONAL REVIEW QUESTIONS

Circle T (true) or F (false)

1. T   F   When God gives an order and men respond, God supplies—even if it takes a miracle.

2. T   F   Jewish feasts, particularly the Passover, held little meaning for Jesus.

3. T   F   At this point in His ministry, Jesus was very popular with the people.

4. T   F   Jesus knew that physical hunger was just as real as spiritual hunger.

5. T   F   Jesus tried to get away from the crowd so He wouldn't have to feed them.

6. T   F   Jesus expected Philip to go to a local grocery store to get food for the crowd.

7. T   F   When the five thousand had been fed, the amount of food God supplied came out to be exactly enough.

8. T   F   If you will take what little bit you have and offer it to God, God will do the multiplication.

9. T   F   God loves to intervene in people's lives and bless them.

10. T   F   God loves those who help others and then don't hang around to get the credit.

MEMORY VERSE

Matthew 4:4 (Memorize, then write it on these lines.)

_____

_____

_____

_____

TRUE OR FALSE ANSWERS:

1-T, 2-F, 3-T, 4-T, 5-F, 6-F, 7-F, 8-T, 9-T, 10-T

NOTES

41

NOTES

Lesson 5
Faith From the Roof
A Paralyzed Man and His Friends

SCRIPTURE: Luke 5:17-26
                (Also Mark 2:3-12; Matthew 9:1-8)
VIDEO REFERENCE: Lesson #5
SUPPLEMENTARY READING REFERENCE:
    The Miracles of Jesus: Then—and Now
    Chapter IV: "Healed by the Faith of Friends"

BIBLE STUDY

1. Jesus Holds a Healing Service

Arriving in Capernaum early one morning, Jesus went immediately to the house of a friend. Within minutes word had spread He was there. People began to gather. Life in the Galilee region was public. Each morning the housekeeper would open her front door as an invitation for friends and neighbors to stop by. The door was shut only at night. The open door meant "Come in." Most of the houses were small, and even though there might be a front courtyard, there was seldom an entrance hall. Visitors, then, came in right off the street.

In no time a crowd had filled the little house, jamming the courtyard as well. The people were eager to hear what Jesus had to say—and to see the miracles which by now occurred every place he went.

In telling the story Mark says, "He preached the word to them."

What do you think Mark meant when he said Jesus "preached the word to them"? (Mark 2:2)

_____ (1) He preached the Bible.

_____ (2) He quoted the Torah—the Old Testament law.

_____ (3) He spoke God's truth for them at that time.

If Jesus didn't have a Bible, and the ancient scrolls were locked up in the synagogues, where do you think He got His sermon material?

_____

_____

Some men came to the healing service bringing a sick friend on a stretcher.

What was wrong with the sick man? (Mark 2:3)

_____

How many men were carrying the stretcher? (Mark 2:3)

_____

Why did they not bring the sick man directly into the house? (Luke 5:18-19)

_____

What did they do with the man on the stretcher? (Mark 2:4)

_____

_____

The typical roof on a Galilean house was almost flat, with just enough slant for water to drain off. Since the houses were open and there was little privacy, the roof was regularly used as a a place of rest and quiet. Many of the houses had an outside stairway leading to the roof, which might be surrounded by a low parapet. On other houses the roof was reached by a ladder.

The roof itself consisted of flat beams laid across the walls of the house, perhaps three feet apart. Brushwood and palm fronds were then put across the beams. Mud, clay, and sod were then put on the brushwood. When they dried, the roof was strong enough to support the weight of several men.

2. **Jesus Forgives Sin**

What so impressed Jesus that He stopped what He was doing to minister to the paralytic? (Matthew 9:2)

_____

The destruction of the roof didn't seem to bother Jesus. He was pleased with these men who laughed at barriers and kept trying until they were able to get their paralyzed friend into Jesus' presence.

What did Jesus call their attitude? (Matthew 9:2)

———— (1) Perserverance

———— (2) Boldness

———— (3) Faith

Whose faith impressed Jesus? (Matthew 9:2)

———— (1) The sick man's faith

———— (2) The faith of his friends

———— (3) The faith of the crowd

On the basis of this faith did Jesus immediately heal the man? (Matthew 9:2, 6)

———— Yes

———— No

What did He do first? (Matthew 9:2)

_____

What did Jesus do before He forgave the man's sins? (Mark 2:5)

———— (1) He asked the man to confess his sins out loud.

———— (2) He led him in the "sinners' prayer."

———— (3) He read him the four spiritual laws and asked the man if he understood them.

———— (4) He asked the man if he wanted to go to heaven when he died.

———— (5) He required the man to be baptized.

———— (6) He made the man renounce all false gods in his life.

———— (7) He told the man to go to confession and do penance.

———— (8) All of the above.

———— (9) None of the above.

Jesus came to reveal a different God than men knew about. He said God was a loving, Heavenly Father. Notice, Jesus did not require anything of the paralytic. He didn't tell him to first confess his sins. He didn't lead him through the "sinner's prayer." He simply looked at him and absolved him of all his sins.

3. Jesus Confounds the Scholars

Who else was present at the miracle service besides Jesus, the sick man and his four friends, and the fans of Jesus? (Matthew 9:3)

_____

We see a great contrast between the mind of Jesus and the minds of the scribes, the Jewish teachers of the law. To the Jews, a sick man was one with whom God was angry. This incident shows how far they had strayed from the mind of God. Jesus' purpose was to reveal God, not to follow their complicated process for forgiving sins. Thus He simply forgave the man's sins.

What were the scribes thinking? (Mark 2:6-7)

_____

_____

_____

What did Jesus call the thoughts of the teachers of the law? (Matthew 9:4)

_____

What two questions did Jesus ask the scribes? (Luke 5:23)

(1)_____

_____

(2)_____

_____

To the Jews a sick man was a man with whom God was angry. They equated all physical suffering with sin.

What did Eliphaz answer when asked two rhetorical questions by Job? (Job 4:7)

Circle T (true) or F (false).

T　　F　　Only the innocent perish.

T　　F　　The upright are never destroyed.

Now we can see why it was imperative for Jesus to forgive the man's sins as a preamble to the miracle about to follow. The man had been raised a Jew. As such he had been taught by the rabbis that his sickness, his paralysis, was the result of some sin he had committed. To have healed him without forgiving his sins would have been more than he could have taken . But once the sin factor was out of the way, he could now accept his healing.

"Son," Jesus said to him tenderly, "God is not angry with you. It's okay." To say your sins are forgiven is to say God is not angry. Jesus was doing what He always did—revealing the Father.

What did He then say to the man? (Mark 2:11)

_____

How did Jesus know these religious teachers were not of God? (3 John 11)

_____

_____

What does the mind of the sinful man produce? (Romans 8:6)

_____

What does the Spirit-controlled mind produce? (Romans 8:6)

(1) _____

(2) _____

How can we we have the mind of Christ? (Romans 8:9)

_____

4. **Jesus Heals Sickness**

   Is healing for the "righteous" only? (Mark 2:17)

   _____ Yes

   _____ No

How did Jesus confirm His authority to forgive sin? (Matthew 9:6)

_____

What did Jesus then tell the man to do? (Matthew 9:6)

_____

How did the people respond to this miracle? (Matthew 9:8)

_____

Do you think Jesus intends for his present day followers to perform similar miracles?

_____ Yes

_____ No

If you answered "yes," what is necessary in order for us to perform the same miracles Jesus performed? (John 14:12)

_____

_____

WRAP UP

Why are miracles needed? If we walk as spiritual people, then why miracles? Why don't we walk in health all the time? Why don't we walk in godly protection all the time? Are miracles only for those who are out there living in horrible sin?

No. Miracles are needed because we are sinful people. We live in a sinful world. We are part of a sinful system. We are part of the natural system which God has set in order, which has been polluted by man as he runs it. Even though I believe God would have us walk as Adam and Eve, in perfect harmony with nature, we don't do it. Because of the evil spirits, because of the Evil One, and because all of us have sinned and come short of the glory of God—we need miracles.

FINAL LESSON

God's people should expect a miracle every day.

PERSONAL REVIEW QUESTIONS

Circle T (true) or F (false)

1. T   F   Only a handful of people witnessed this miracle.

2. T   F   The Holy Spirit gave Jesus the ability to know the thoughts of the scribes.

3. T   F   The teachers of the law were more concerned with correct doctrine than they were with man's suffering.

4. T   F   Jesus told the man He would not heal him unless he first paid for the roof.

5. T   F   Jesus was upset because His church service had been interrupted.

6. T   F   It was because of the faith of the man's friends that Jesus was able to heal the paralytic.

7. T   F   This kind of faith for healing is still present in the world.

8. T   F   When you are sick it is a sign God is angry with you.

9. T   F   Jesus told the paralyzed man he must confess his sins before he could be healed.

10. T   F   The scribes tried to trap Jesus; instead, He trapped them.

11. T   F   All miracles have God's reason behind them.

12. T   F   Miracles are needed because we are sinful people, living in a sinful world.

MEMORY VERSE

John 14:12 (Memorize, then write it on these lines.)

_____

_____

_____

_____

NOTES

TRUE OR FALSE ANSWERS:

1-F, 2-T, 3-T, 4-F, 5-F, 6-T, 7-T, 8-F, 9-F, 10-T, 11-T, 12-T

49

NOTES

Lesson 6
A Demon Possessed Boy
"Everything is possible for him who believes."

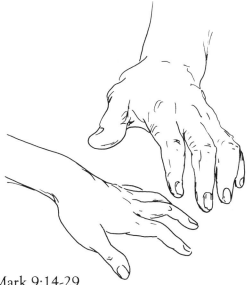

SCRIPTURE: Mark 9:14-29
> (Also Matthew 17:14-21 and Luke 9:37-43)

VIDEO REFERENCE: Lesson 6

SUPPLEMENTARY READING REFERENCE:
> *The Miracles of Jesus: Then—and Now*
> Chapter IX: "Power to Cast Out Evil Spirits"

BIBLE STUDY

1. The Place

This miracle took place at the base of Mt. Hermon on the Lebanese border in northern Israel. Snow-capped most of the year, Mt Hermon towers 9101 feet above sea level as an Israeli sentinal between Israel on the south and Lebanon and Syria on the north and east. Its melting snow cap provides the water for the Jordan River which fills the beautiful blue Sea of Galilee and later empties into the Dead Sea at the lowest spot on the surface of the earth. In his beautiful psalm of unity, David said unity among men was "as if the dew of Hermon were falling on Mt. Zion" (Psalm 133:3).

2. The Occasion

Jesus had just descended from a brief stay on the high slopes of the mountain. Three of His disciples, Peter, James, and John—His "inner circle"—had climbed the mountain with Him. As the four men prayed two of the ancient prophets—long dead—had appeared. Then God spoke directly to Jesus, as the disciples listened.

What happened to Jesus as He prayed on the mountaintop? (Mark 9:2)

What were the names of the two prophets who appeared? (Mark 9:4)

_____

_____

What was Peter's reaction? (Mark 9:5)

_____

_____

_____

3. **The Problem**

While Jesus and His three friends were on the mountain, significant events were occuring in the valley below.

What were the other disciples doing? (Mark 9:14)

_____

_____

Earlier Jesus had called His disciples together and told them how to deal with crisis situations.

What had He given them power and authority to do? (Luke 9:1)

(1)_____

(2)_____

Had the disciples been able to carry out that earlier commission? (Luke 9:6)

_____ Yes

_____ No

It was in the valley, at the base of Mt.Hermon, that Jesus came face to face with a situation that demanded a miracle—a miracle of deliverance.

What was the cause of the boy's problem? (Mark 9:17)

_____

What was the evil spirit making the boy do? (Mark 9:17-18)

(1) _____

(2) _____

(3) _____

(4) _____

(5) _____

Matthew adds that the seizures caused by the demon had all the symptoms of a particular disease. Although this disease is not always caused by demons, demons often make people act in a way that has the appearances of that disease.

What is the disease? (Matthew 17:15)

_____

When the boy was afflicted with seizures what did the demons make him do? (Matthew 17:15)

(1) _____

(2) _____

The disciples, who had earlier been given power and authority to deal with these kinds of things, had ministered to the boy.

What was the result of the disciples' ministry? (Mark 9:18)

_____

4. **The Demon Defeated**

How would you describe Jesus' reaction to the powerlessness of the people in dealing with demons? (Mark 9:19)

(Check all right answers)

_____ (1) Understanding

_____ (2) Exasperation

_____ (3) Anger

_____ (4) Patience

_____ (5) Frustration

_____ (6) Aggravation

What did Jesus tell the father to do? (Mark 9:19)

_____

When the boy was brought to Jesus the evil spirit, sensing Jesus' authority, responded violently.

What did the demon make the boy do? (Mark 9:20)

(1)_____

(2)_____

(3)_____

(4)_____

How long had the demon been in the boy? (Mark 9:21

_____

What did the boy's father ask Jesus? (Mark 9:22)

_____

_____

Jesus responded in a strange way to the father's statement. The father had said to Jesus, "If you can do anything. . ." Jesus turned the question back to the father, indicating the father's faith was all that was necessary to set the boy free.

What did Jesus say was possible to anyone who believes in the power of God? (Mark 9:23)

_____

Jesus is dealing with a universal truth. He is saying that faith resides in the individual. If you have faith, you can do it. . . It's an exciting approach to life. Our problem is our lack of faith. The cure for your boy, Jesus says, depends not on Me, but on you. To approach anything with a spirit of hopelessness makes it hopeless. Any time you say a thing is impossible, it becomes impossible.

What was the father's response to Jesus statement on faith? (Mark 9:24)

_____

_____

Suddenly something blazes up inside the father."I believe!" he exclaims. It's a kind of a "Wow! I do believe!" Then he adds "Help me overcome my unbelief."

In other words, I don't ever want to go back to where I was. I don't ever want to drop back down to the old level of seeing things from the natural. From now on I want to remain where I am right now—seeing things from the supernatural.

Why did the father believe in the power of God?

_____ (1) Because he saw a miracle.

_____ (2) Because he believed what Jesus said.

What was the name of the demon? (Mark 9:25)

_____

Luke sums up what happened here in a few words.

List the three things Jesus did. (Luke 9:42)

1. _____

2. _____

3. _____

5. **The Source of Power**

If we do not stay "plugged in" to our source of power, we—like the disciples—will fail, no matter how many talents God has given us.

Where did Jehoshaphat, king of Judah, look for help to defeat his enemies? (2 Chronicles 20:12)

_____

In Psalm 34: 1-3 David said we should:

(1) bless the Lord at all times,

(2) let praise constantly fill our mouth,

(3) boast in the Lord

(4) rejoice even when afflicted

(5) glorify the Lord

(6) exalt his name together

When we do this how will God respond? (Psalm 34:4)

(1)_____

(2)_____

David also said, in Psalm 103:1-2, we should:

(1) Let our innermost being praise God's holy name

(2) forget not all God's benefits

What are the benefits of God? (Psalm 103:3-5)

(1)_____

(2)_____

(3)_____

(4)_____

(5)_____

_____

What is the source of power Jesus told the disciples they lacked? (Mark 9:29)

_____

WRAP UP

So Jesus says this kind can come out only through prayer, or, as some versions of the Bible say, prayer and fasting. What was He talking about? Jesus didn't stop to pray, or to fast. He didn't say, "Wait here, I'll be back in three days after I've fasted and prayed." He just spoke the word and the demon left.

Remember, though, Jesus had just come down from the mountain where He had been praying and fasting. He had not been praying and fasting for this little boy. He didn't even know the child was down there, waiting for Him. Jesus lived a "fasted life." Like Paul, He prayed constantly. He was always in touch with God about everything. He was not only prepared to give up food, He was prepared to give up His very life. He lived a cross life, a life of constant sacrifice. No demon can withstand that kind of life. No wonder when He spoke, the demon had to leave.

So Jesus says to His disciples, "You don't live close enough to God. If you lived close enough to God, you would be equipped with power." God gives us gifts, but they are useless unless we use them for Him.

FINAL LESSONS

What we do in private, in our relationship with God, is more important than what we do in public. If we do things in private in our relationship with God, God will use us in public ministry elsewhere. All He requires is that we remain close to Him.

PERSONAL REVIEW QUESTIONS

Circle T (true) or F (false)

1. T F One of the purposes of going aside to pray is to make us more effective when we meet people who need ministry.

2. T F Jesus was proud of His disciples for the way they were handling the argumentative scribes.

3. T F The helplessness of the disciples gave the scribes an opportunity to sneer at Jesus.

4. T F Jesus never turned away from human need.

5. T F The demon was not able to recognize Jesus as the Son of God.

6. T F Demons love to torment helpless people.

7. T F We don't need to call upon experts in healing; we have that power and authority ourselves when Christ is in us.

8. T F Faith is a gift from God.

9. T F Some demons come out easily, some don't.

10. T F The evil spirit in the boy came out quietly.

11. T F If we fast and pray, we too can take authority over the most firmly entrenched evil spirit.

MEMORY VERSE

Mark 9:23 (Memorize, then write it on these lines.)

_____

_____

_____

_____

TRUE OR FALSE ANSWERS

1-T, 2-F, 3-T, 4-T, 5-F, 6-T, 7-T, 8-T, 9-T, 10-F, 11-T

NOTES

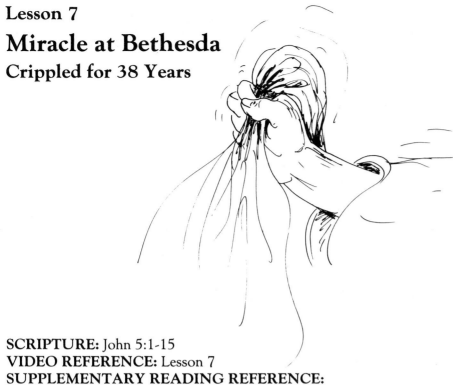

Lesson 7
Miracle at Bethesda
Crippled for 38 Years

SCRIPTURE: John 5:1-15
VIDEO REFERENCE: Lesson 7
SUPPLEMENTARY READING REFERENCE:
The Miracles of Jesus: Then—and Now
Chapter V: "Healing Through the Spoken Word"

1. The Setting

Jesus was apparently alone when He arrived in Jerusalem to attend the feast of Pentecost. It was a long walk from His home in Capernaum to Jerusalem— a distance of about 110 miles. It was late spring and temperatures in the desert regions in the Jordan valley would have been already soaring to 100 degrees F. The walk from Jericho, near the Dead Sea, to Jerusalem—a distance of almost 30 miles, is one of the steepest ascents in the world, through one of the most forboding sections of the world—the Judean wilderness.

Arriving in Jerusalem, He went straight to a favorite place of rest and refreshment, the Pool of Bethesda near the Sheep Gate of the city wall. The name Bethesda means, literally, "house of outpouring," or "house of mercy." The name was significant, not simply because this was a delightful resting place for residents and travelers alike, but because of the medicinal qualities of the waters which may have originated with a hot sulphur spring that bubbled out of the ground. Actually, there were two pools—an upper pool where the hot water bubbled in from underground, and a much deeper, adjoining pool where people could actually dive in and swim. The pools were surrounded by five covered colonnades or tiled porches.

Not only would weary travelers gather under the roofs of these porches, but a large number of sick people came here to bathe in the waters. The day Jesus arrived He found the place crowded with a number of disabled people—the blind, the lame, the paralyzed. The original text of John's biography does not include the latter part of verse three and verse four, which I have included in brackets. This seems to have been added later as an explanation of why these sick people came to the pool. It was a common saying that the "moving of the waters" was caused by an angel who came down and troubled the waters. Actually there was, beneath the pool, a hot,

59

subterranean stream which every now and then bubbled up and disturbed the waters of the upper pool. When this happened the people would rush for the water to take advantage of its medicinal value.

2. **Jesus Seeks the Individual**

In His parables and by His actions Jesus makes it clear that He is not interested in crowds, but in each person.

To what does He compare someone who is estranged from Him? (Matthew 18:12-14)

_____

There were many sick people lying beside the Pool of Bethesda.

Why did Jesus seek out only one of them? (John 12:49)

_____

3. **Jesus Gives His Holy Spirit**

In another place Jesus made a spiritual reference to water bubbling out of an underground spring. He said the Holy Spirit in us was like a refreshing spring.

What kind of water will flow from such a person? (John 7:38)

_____

How can we tap into that source? (John 7:38)

_____

What did Jesus refer to as "living water"? (John 7:39)

_____

How can we receive the Holy Spirit? (Luke 11:9-13)

_____

_____

What will be the result of our being baptized in the Holy Spirit? (Acts 1:8)

_____

_____

4. Conditions for Healing

How long had the begger been paralyzed? (John 5:5)

_____

Why did Jesus ask the man if he wanted to be healed? (John 5:6)
(Check all the right answers.)

_____ (1) Jesus wasn't sure He could heal him.

_____ (2) All the other people around the pool had tried to help him but had failed.

_____ (3) Jesus wanted to find out if the man liked his sickness more than he wanted to be healed.

_____ (4) The man would have to give up his Social Security checks if he let Jesus heal him.

_____ (5) Jesus wanted to find out if the man was willing to designate his Social Security checks to the Jesus Evangelistic Association.

_____ (6) The desire to be healed is a prerequisite to healing.

Regardless of the man's whiny attitude, how did Jesus—who was God—know he was ready for a miracle of healing? (1 Samuel 16:7)

_____

5. The Word of God in Healing

All that is ever necessary for healing—whether it is healing for a broken heart or a crippled body—is a word from God.

There are many healing procedures found in the Bible.

What procedure is to be used according to James 5:14-15?

_____

_____

_____

What procedure did Jesus use in John 9:6-7?

_____

_____

What did Jesus do in Matthew 8:3?

_____

_____

How did Jesus heal in Luke 17:11-14?

_____

_____

What did Jesus say brought the healing in Matthew 9:20-22?

_____

_____

There seem to be as many procedures for healing as their are situations; yet one common thread runs through every situation—the word of God is spoken.

By what means are we able to heal today? (Acts 3:16)

_____

_____

6. **Dealing With the Man**

Who did the man blame for his condition? (John 5:7)

_____ (1) His parents who had sinned.

_____ (2) God, who made him crippled.

_____ (3) The folks around the pool who wouldn't help him into the water.

_____ (4) Jesus, for not arriving earlier.

_____ (5) He took the blame himself.

_____ (6) He didn't blame anyone.

Did Jesus condemn the beggar for his ignorance?

_____ Yes

_____ No

What did Jesus do before he healed the beggar? (John 5:7-8)
(Check one answer)

_____ (1) He said He would go ahead and heal the man on the condition he agreed to enroll in Peter's Tuesday night Bible study.

_____ (2) He made the man renounce his belief that the angels came and stirred up the water.

_____ (3) He led the man in a series of prayers of repentence and confession.

_____ (4) He took the man to one side and led him through inner healing to get rid of all the bitterness he held toward the people who had not helped him.

_____ (5) He simply spoke the word and healed him.

When a Roman military commander, deeply concerned about his servant who was at home, paralyzed and in terrible pain, came to Jesus begging for help, he understood how Jesus healed.

What did the military commander ask Jesus to do? (Matthew 8:8)

_____

_____

Where do we find the word of faith which heals? (Romans 10:8)

(1) _____

(2) _____

7. Problems

After he was healed, the man was grilled by the Jewish legalists who were upset because they saw the man carrying his mat on the Sabbath—which was supposed to be a day of rest.

What did the law say about the Sabbath day? (Exodus 20:8)

_____

_____

Did Jesus violate that law when He healed on the Sabbath? (Mark 2:27)

_____ Yes

_____ No

The man, puzzled about the whole thing and not sure why everyone wasn't rejoicing, refused to make an explanation to the Jews.

Who did he blame for his breaking the sabbath? (John 5:11)

_____

Why wasn't the man able to identify Jesus? (John 5:13)

_____

_____

What did Jesus tell the man the next time He saw him? (John 5:14)

_____

What do you think Jesus meant when He said "stop sinning"? (John 5:14)

_____ (1) The man had been stealing money.

_____ (2) The man was still blaming others—including Jesus—for his troubles.

_____ (3) The man has failed to report his healing to the Israeli Medical Association.

Does this mean God would withdraw His grace? Not at all. Did it mean Jesus would take away the man's healing? Of course not. It did mean, however, that the man would make himself sick again—and this time the condition would be even worse—if he did not start giving God the glory and taking responsibility (not credit) for his healing.

WRAP UP

Miracles occur to show men that the Kingdom of God is here. Present. It is a silent Kingdom operating in this universe. Without miracles there is no proof that God is any bigger than we are. We need miracles to show men that there is a God "out there" who not only created us, but who cares for us—and is still in control of all the natural laws.

FINAL LESSON

How does God heal today? He will heal anyone on the basis of His mercy. But there is great evidence He prefers to heal on the basis of inheritance. God wants to use us to heal others. God wants His miracles to come through us.

PERSONAL REVIEW QUESTIONS

Circle T (true) or F (false)

1. T   F   It doesn't matter whether a person wants to get well—Jesus in His compassion will heal him anyway.

2. T   F   The spoken word of faith, in the heart and mouth of a believer, brings healing.

3. T   F   It takes a lot of faith to be healed by God.

4. T   F   God heals the just and the unjust.

5. T   F   You have the right to receive the word of God when it comes into your life, and be healed.

6. T   F   Miracles occur to show men that the Kingdom of God is here now.

7.　T　F　Without miracles there is no proof that God is any bigger than we are.

8.　T　F　Miracles are for those who demand them.

9.　T　F　You have the power, through Christ, to heal others.

10.　T　F　If we are baptized in the Holy Spirit, we are automatically healed of all our diseases.

MEMORY VERSE

Romans 10:8 (Memorize, then write it on these lines)

_____

_____

_____

_____

TRUE OR FALSE ANSWERS:

1-F, 2-T, 3-F, 4-T, 5-T, 6-T, 7-T, 8-F, 9-T, 10-F

NOTES

Lesson 8
Sight for Blind Eyes
Miracle At the Pool of Siloam

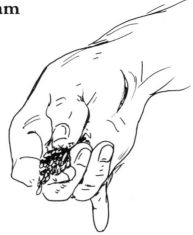

SCRIPTURE: John 9:1-38
VIDEO REFERENCE: Lesson 8
SUPPLEMENTARY READING REFERENCE:
 The Miracles of Jesus: Then—and Now
 Chapter VI: "Sight for Blind Eyes"

Miracle, basically, is the intervention of a higher law over a lower law. God has, in the creation of this earth, set in motion certain physical laws that govern this universe. There are laws of psychology and human behavior, laws of health, laws of physics, laws of engineering—many different kinds of laws.

But there are other laws that are invisible to us; that are visible only to God, that control the Kingdom of Heaven. Miracle is basically the imposition of the laws of the Kingdom of Heaven over the laws of this world.

BIBLE STUDY

1. Miracles of Healing

Jesus healed a number of blind people while He was on earth.

Why did He pay attention to the two blind men in Galilee? (Matthew 9:27-28)

(1) _____
(2) _____

What was Jesus' question to these blind men? (Matthew 9:28)

_____
_____

How did He heal them? (Matthew 9:29)

_____ (1) He spit in their eyes.

_____ (2) He told them to go dip in the River Jordan.

_____ (3) He told them to go to the priest and be cleansed.

_____ (4) He touched their eyes.

To what did Jesus attribute their healing? (Matthew 9:29)

_____ (1) That they nor their parents had ever sinned.

_____ (2) That they loved their fathers and mothers.

_____ (3) That both had great faith.

_____ (4) None of the above.

The story we are studying today is the only miracle in the Gospels in which the sufferer is said to have been afflicted from birth. The Book of Acts tells of two other miracles concerning people helpless from birth.

What were the afflictions of those who received these miraculous healings?

(1) (Acts 3:1-10) _____

(2) (Acts 14:8) _____

2. **Jesus' Disciples**

The disciples had no interest in the man's blindness. Blindness was common in the days of Jesus due to the high rate of eye disease—a condition that still exists in the desert regions of the Middle East. The disciples were interested in the theology behind his blindness. They simply saw this as a good time to get an answer to a question which had bothered Jews since the time of Job—a problem which remains to this day: Who is responsible for affliction?

The disciples of Jesus, like most Jews, believed all suffering was the result of someone's sin.

Whom did they therefore suspect was responsible for this man's blindness? (John 9:2)

(1) _____

(2) _____

According to Jewish interpretation of certain Old Testament passages, how could they have assumed his blindness was a result of sin?

Exodus 20:5 _____

_____

Exodus 34:7, Numbers 14:18 _____

_____

_____

_____

Although this was the law of the Old Testament, God knew we could not continue to live under that kind of curse.

What did God do to set us free? (Romans 8:2-3)

_____

_____

_____

How does Christ redeem us from the curse of the law? (Galatians 3:13)

_____

_____

_____

3. **Jesus, the Son of God**

Jesus said this man's blindness was not caused by the sins of his parents or his own sin.

Why was he blind? (John 9:3)

_____

_____

Why did Jesus get involved with the blind man? (John 9:4-5)

_____

_____

_____

The primary purpose of the healings and miracles was the glorification of God.

Remember, miracles are the exhibition of one law overriding another law. In this case, it is not only the imposition of the higher law of love over the physical law that says once a man is permanently blind he remains that way, but Jesus went a step beyond and overrode the religious laws of the day.

How did Jesus break the religious law? (John 9:14)

_____

_____

4. The Miracle

Jesus could have healed the man by simply speaking, or he could have healed him by touching his eyes.

What did Jesus do? (John 9:6)

_____

_____

By making mud on the Sabbath, which was forbidden by Jewish law, He deliberately offended the religious officials of the day—the Pharisees.

What did He then tell the man to do? (John 9:7)

_____

_____

The Pool of Siloam dated back to the year 701 BC when Jerusalem was under seige by the Assyrian king, Sennacherib.

Where did the water from the pool come from? (II Chronicles 32:30)

_____

What was the name of the King who built the tunnel under the wall to let the water flow into the city? (II Chronicles 32:1-4, II Kings 20:20)

_____

In the days of Jesus the Pool of Siloam was also called "Sent."

What do you think that term meant? (John 9:7)

_____ (1) Jesus *sent* the blind man to wash there.

_____ (2) The Jews bottled the water and *sent* it to their friends.

_____ (3) The water was *sent* from the Gihon Spring outside the wall, through Hezekiah's tunnel, into the pool.

_____ (4) The meaning of the word has been lost.

The religious Jews always went through ceremonial washing before they ate. They also filled ceremonial urns with water and poured that water on the ground during the Feast of Tabernacles. This water was drawn from the Pool of Siloam. On one occasion Jesus stood up during the Feast of Tabernacles and chided the Jews about their water ceremonies.

What did Jesus say about water? (John 7:37-38)

_____

_____

_____

To whom was He referring? (John 7:39)

_____

By sending the blind man to the Pool of Siloam, from which the ceremonial water was drawn, he was illustrating what He had said at the Feast of Tabernacles.

What was Jesus proving?

_____ (1) There was healing power in the water.

_____ (2) He expected Jews to be ceremonially cleansed before they could be healed.

_____ (3) He was showing the healing came from the Holy Spirit, not the water.

There was one significant difference in the ceremonial washing and the washing the blind man did. When the Jews washed with ceremonial water they remained the same. When this man washed, he came up seeing. The difference was the touch of Jesus.

5. The Pharisees

Although Jesus commended the Pharisees for their dedication to the law, He was quick to point out they had missed the real point of the law by adhering to the letter of the law while having no idea of the spirit in which it was given. They knew the law, but not the lawgiver.

What were the "weightier matters of the law" the Pharisees neglected, while majoring on the letter of the law? (Matthew 23:23)

(1) _____

(2) _____

(3) _____

They were more interested in keeping the law than glorifying God. They had made an idol of the Sabbath, bowing down to it and believing it was more important to keep the law concerning the Sabbath than to help someone in need.

What did Jesus say about the Sabbath? (Mark 2:27)

_____

_____

To the Pharisees, the law was more important than human kind. When they found a woman committing adultery they wanted to act on the basis of the law rather than the basis of forgiveness.

What did the Pharisees want to do to the guilty woman? (John 8:3-5)

_____

What did Jesus tell the Pharisees? (John 8:7)

_____

_____

What did Jesus tell the guilty woman? (John 8:11)

(1) _____

(2) _____

Why did the Pharisees say Jesus was not from God? (John 9:16)

_____

_____

What did Jesus say about the Pharisees' actions toward God? (Matthew 15:9)

(1) _____

(2) _____

What did He call the Pharisees?

Matthew 15:7 _____

Matthew 23:27 _____

_____

What did He say the Pharisees were full of? (Matthew 23:28)

(1) _____

(2) _____

6. **The Blind Man's Parents**

    Why were his parents afraid to tell the Pharisees why the man could now see? (John 9:22)

    _____

7. **Spiritual Blindness**

    What argument did the blind man use when told to deny Jesus was from God? (John 9:25)

    _____

    _____

    _____

    What did the Pharisees do when the man refused to deny that Jesus healed him? (John 9:34)

    _____

When Jesus told the man He was the Messiah, how did the man respond? (John 9:38)

_____

Who were the real blind men? (John 9:40-41)

_____

Now that we know Him and His healing power, what should we expect? (Luke 12:48b)

_____

_____

_____

WRAP UP

Jesus points out that knowledge demands action. Unto whom much is given much is required. God requires we give what we have received—testimony of our own healing.

PERSONAL REVIEW QUESTIONS

Circle T (true) or F (false)

1. T F The man was blind because his parents sinned.

2. T F The question was not really who was at fault, but who was going to do something about it.

3. T F The blind man didn't know who Jesus was.

4. T F Jesus said, "I am the light of the world."

5. T F The man was called a beggar because he had to beg Jesus to heal him.

6. T F It was not just Jesus' spit that gave the man his sight, but the man's willingness to obey Jesus by washing in the pool.

7. T F The Pharisees thought Jesus was spiritual because He healed on the Sabbath.

8. T F Once the man could see, he believed Jesus was a prophet.

9. T F The man's parents were afraid of the Jews.

10. T F The Pharisees were eager to hear, over and over, how Jesus healed the man because they wanted to become His disciples.

11. T   F   God wants us to keep the letter of His law, regardless of who gets hurt.

12. T   F   God requires that we give testimony of our own healing, and then— in Jesus' name—we are to give healing to others.

MEMORY VERSE

John 7:38 (Memorize, then write it on these lines.)

_____

_____

_____

_____

TRUE AND FALSE ANSWERS:

1-F, 2-T, 3-T, 4-T, 5-F, 6-T, 7-F, 8-T, 9-T, 10-F, 11-F, 12-T

NOTES

Lesson 9

The Leper
Hope for the Hopeless

SCRIPTURE: Luke 5:12-14
(Also Mark 1:40-45; Matthew 8:1-4)
VIDEO REFERENCE: Lesson 9
SUPPLEMENTARY READING REFERENCE:
The Miracles of Jesus: Then and Now
Chapter VII: "Hope for the Hopeless"

No disease in history has separated the patient from society as has leprosy. The leper was hated by others, believed himself to be hated by God, and so hated himself.

It was such a man who came to Jesus, asking for help.

1. The Leper Approaches Jesus

In Jesus' day leprosy was called "the living death." It is one of the most terrible diseases of all times. No other sickness—except for the new disease of AIDS—can draw life from a person with such calculated cruelty, resulting in oozing sores, loss of body parts, and eventual death.

Lepers not only suffered from the physical pain of the disease, but the Levitical law demanded a person show himself to a priest at the first signs of the disease. If it was determined he had leprosy he was forced to submit to the Jewish law.

List six things the leper was forced to do. (Leviticus 13:45-46)

(1) _____

(2) _____

(3) _____

(4) _____

(5) _____

(6) _____

As horrible as the physical disease was, the emotional destruction was equally great. Banished. Unclean. Defiled. Declared spiritually dead. The leper was compelled to leave his home and friends and wander in the darkness with other lepers, covering his face, warning anyone who came close with his hoarse cry "Unclean! Unclean!"

In Jesus' day, the rules regarding lepers had multiplied from the simple regulations set forth in Leviticus. The leper was barred from Jerusalem and all walled towns. The Law listed 61 different contacts which could defile the proper Jew. Being touched by, or touching a leper was second only to touching a dead body. If a leper put his head through the door or window of any house or building, that building was declared "unclean"—even to the roof beams. It was illegal to greet or speak to a leper. No one might come closer than six feet (four cubits). If a leper was upwind from a Jew he had to stand at least 150 feet away. People, including the rabbis, often threw stones at the lepers, much as they would at a mangy dog, to keep them away.

Lepers often fell into a hopelessness that destroyed their desire to get well. The sickness destroyed not only the body but the attitudes of the mind. The leper in this story, however, had a different attitude.

What was the first thing the leper did when he saw Jesus? (Matthew 8:2)

_____

What did he say to Jesus? (Matthew 8:2)

_____

Unlike many of the lepers in Jesus' time, this man had a rather mild case of the disease. (Luke 5:12)

_____ True

_____ False

2. Jesus Reaches Out

That a man, any man, should touch a leper was as unthinkable as a man reaching down to pick up a poisonous snake by the tail. Yet it was exactly these two signs that God had given Moses 1200 years before when He called him to return to Egypt and lead his people into freedom.

What was the first thing God told Moses to do? (Exodus 4:1-5)

_____

_____

_____

Describe the second thing God told Moses to do. (Exodus 4:6-8)

_____

_____

_____

The serpent was the symbol of danger. Leprosy was the symbol of disease. As easily as God could perform these signs, so He could protect from danger and heal disease. Jesus did this when He did the unthinkable and touched the leper.

What happened when Jesus touched the leper? (Matthew 8:3)

_____

3. Beyond the Law

One of Jesus' major purposes in life was to help the hopeless. Thus if the law of Moses brought hopelessness, Jesus overrode it with the law of love.

If Jesus was not breaking the Law, then what was He doing? (Matthew 5:17)

_____

What made Jesus think He could do this? (Matthew 28:18)

_____

_____

After healing the leper, what did Jesus tell the man to do? (Matthew 8:4)

_____ (1) Go home and tell his neighbors.

_____ (2) Tell no man.

_____ (3) Follow him as a disciple.

_____ (4) Have his agent submit a resume to the Christian television stations as a possible guest.

_____ (5) Submit himself to the priests and make an offering in the temple as required by the law.

How do you explain that Jesus was willing to break the law of Moses by touching the leper, yet commanded the man to keep the law which required him to return to the priest to have his healing verified?

_____

_____

_____

Describe the procedure the priest was to go through if he found a man healed of leprosy. (Leviticus 14:1-7)

_____

_____

_____

Why did Jesus tell the man to go to the priest? (Matthew 8:4)

_____

At the beginning of His ministry, Jesus pointed out that leprosy was normally incurable. He had stood in the synagogue at Nazareth, reading from the prophet Isaiah, proclaiming Himself the Messiah. In His explanation to the people, He said only one man in Hebrew history had been healed of leprosy.

What was that man's name? (Luke 4:27).

_____

What had Elisha required that man, the king of Syria, to do in order to be healed? (2 Kings 5:14)

_____

_____

Jesus told this story to the Jews in Nazareth in order to let them know He had the same power as Elisha.

How did the people respond? (Luke 4:28-29)

_____

_____

How did Jesus escape? (Luke 4:30)

_____

_____

Why did Jesus risk His life to heal this leper? (Mark 10:45)

_____

_____

Although leprosy, now known as Hansen's Disease, is virtually wiped out in the western world, a new—and equally dreaded disease, AIDS—is now at epidemic levels.

Is it possible for Jesus to heal AIDS just as He healed leprosy? (Mark 11:22-24)

_____ Yes

_____ No

Do we have God's protection as well as His authority when we minister healing to the sick? (Mark 16:17-18)

_____ Yes

_____ No

WRAP UP

Christians must run the risk of infection by ministering to those who come for help. Remember, Jesus promises protection (Mark 16:18) if we are forced to handle snakes or drink poison. As Jesus touched this leper, so God's people are called to reach out and touch *all* who are hopeless. Healing comes when we are willing to lay down our lives for others.

FINAL LESSON

Healings, today, should be confirmed by proper authorities—either spiritual authorities or medical people. Testimony is needed that the God of miracles is still touching people and healing them.

PERSONAL REVIEW QUESTIONS

Circle T (true) or F (false).

1. T F Compassion means suffering with the sufferer.

2. T F No disease in history has separated the patient from society as has leprosy.

3. T F Leprosy is the only disease God could not heal.

4. T F The leper who came to Jesus didn't think Jesus could really heal him.

5. T F Jewish law was not important to Jesus.

6. T F To Jesus, the law of love took precedence over all other rules and regulations.

7. T F Christians must run the risk of infection by ministering to those who come for help.

8. T F Jesus was afraid of the Jewish priests, which is the reason He told the leper not to tell about his healing.

9. T F The main reason we should believe in God is so we can be healthy.

10. T F It's wrong to pray for God to heal AIDS since doctors say it is incurable.

11. T F Christians should not be afraid to have their doctors confirm their healing.

12. T F God loves to heal all diseased people.

MEMORY VERSE

Mark 11:24 (Memorize, then write it on these lines.)

_____

_____

_____

_____

_____

TRUE OR FALSE ANSWERS:

1-T, 2-T, 3-F, 4-F, 5-F, 6-T, 7-T, 8-F, 9-F, 10-F, 11-T, 12-T

NOTES

Lesson 10

Lazarus

"If you had been here, my brother would not have died."

SCRIPTURE: John 11:1-44
VIDEO REFERENCE: Lesson 10
SUPPLEMENTARY READING REFERENCE:
   The Miracles of Jesus: Then—and Now
   Chapter X: "Power Over Death"

1. Prelude to a Miracle

Three months before this miracle took place, during the Jewish celebration of Hanukkah, Jesus had been in Jerusalem. A large number of people had followed Him, listening to His teachings, observing His miracles.

What did they want to know about Jesus? (John 10:24)

_____

_____

What was Jesus' two-fold answer? (John 10:25)

(1)_____

(2)_____

_____

Why were the people unwilling to accept His answers? (John 10:26)

_____

_____

Who did Jesus say He identified with? (John 10:30)

_____

_____

How did the Jews react to Jesus' answers to their question? (John 10:31)

_____

What was their reason for wanting to kill Jesus? (John 10:33)

_____

_____

_____

Escaping from the angry mob Jesus left Jerusalem and went to the village of Bethabara near the place where John the Baptist had stayed before he was executed.

Where was Bethabara located? (John 10:40)

_____

2. **Setting for a Miracle**

For several weeks Jesus had been on the eastern side of the Jordan River in the region of Peraea, probably in the little village of Bethabara. Most of His time there had been spent teaching. Then a messenger from Jerusalem arrived, saying His friend, Lazarus, was _muy grave_—gravely ill. Lazarus lived with his two sisters in a small village on the Mount of Olives just outside the wall of the city of Jerusalem.

What was the name of the village? (John 11:1)

_____

What were the names of Lazarus' sisters? (John 11:1-2)

(1)_____

(2)_____

Deeply concerned that their brother was dying, the sisters sent desperate word to Jesus who was almost a day's journey away—begging Him to come. They knew He had the power to heal the sick. They knew if He would come, Lazarus would be well again.

What was Jesus' response to the message? (John 11:4)

_____

_____

_____

How long did Jesus wait before going to Bethany? (John 11:6)

_____

Why do you think Jesus waited, rather than responding immediately to the cry for help?

(Check the right answers)

_____ (1) He was afraid to return to the area of Jersualem

_____ (2) He knew if He returned to Jerusalem He would be arrested and executed—and His time had not yet come.

_____ (3) Lazarus was going to die anyway—and He didn't want to be there when it happened.

_____ (4) He knew His Father had something bigger in mind than healing.

_____ (5) Jesus did only what His Father told Him to do.

_____ (6) Jesus had no intention of responding to the emotional request of two hysterical women.

When Jesus finally decided it was time to return to Bethany, His disciples objected.

What were His disciples afraid of? (John 11:8)

_____

Which disciple was brave enough to say, "Let us also go, that we may die with Him?" (John 11:16)

_____

Did Jesus know ahead of time that Lazarus had already died? (John 11:11-14)

_____ Yes

_____ No

_____ He suspected he was dead but wasn't sure.

3. **Arrival in Bethany**

Who was the first one to meet Jesus when He arrived in Bethany? (John 11:20)

_____

How long had Lazarus been dead? (John 11:17)

_____

What was Martha's attitude toward Jesus? (John 11:21)

(Check the right answers)

_____ (1) Anger and exasperation

_____ (2) Faith

_____ (3) Discouragement

_____ (4) Hopelessness

Did Martha understand that Jesus intended to raise her brother from the grave? (John 11:24)

_____ Yes

_____ No

Where was Martha's faith? (John ll:27)

_____ (1) In the resurrection process.

_____ (2) In Jesus ability to raise her brother from the dead.

_____ (3) In Jesus as the Son of God.

Name three other people who had previously discovered Jesus was the Messiah.

John 1:41 _____

John 9:35-38 _____

Matthew 16:16 _____

4. Eternal Life

Among the Jews, only the Pharisees had any concept of life after death. Yet the best they could come up with was some kind of dark and undefined belief that there was life after death. They thought that by keeping the law they would rise from the dead.

Nearly all the Old Testament writers had some kind of belief in life after death. The first to believe in a personal resurrection from the dead was Job. His belief stemmed from a question he asked.

What was Job's question? (Job 14:14)

_____

_____

What did Job come to believe as a result of asking that question? (Job 19:25-27)

About his Redeemer: _____

_____

About his body: _____

_____

About life after death: _____

_____

_____

The best the Jews could come up with, with their limited revelation, was the concept of a a shadowy place after death called "Sheol." Sheol was neither heaven nor hell, but an abode of the dead. When you died you didn't disappear, you went to Sheol. David had a good bit to say about Sheol.

Who did David say he would find in Sheol? (Psalm 139:8)

_____

In another place in the Psalms David used the same word for the home of the righteous after death that Jesus used.

Where did David feel he was going after death? (Psalm 73:25)

_____

5. The Miracle

Lazarus' tomb was a natural cave in deep rock, winding down several levels to a grave site where the body was placed about 30 feet below the surface. Once the body had been prepared and placed in the cave, a rock was rolled over the opening, sealing it to keep out the wild animals and flesh-eating birds of prey.

Jesus stood before the tomb, listening to the people mourning and weeping. He responded emotionally.

What did Jesus do at the tomb of Lazarus? (John 11:35)

_____

Jesus gave us a picture of a God who cares. Paul amplifies that picture in Ephesians 2:4-7.

Why, according to Paul, does God offer us eternal life? (Ephesians 2:4)

_____

Practical Martha could think of only one thing: the grim, repulsive, putrefying corpse of her brother. Jews believed that the spirit of the departed hovered around the tomb for four days, seeking some way to re-enter the body. At the end of four days, however, when the body was so decayed it was no longr recognizable, the spirit departed for Sheol. Understanding that gives even deeper meaning to the words of Jesus to the criminal who was dying beside him on the cross.

When did Jesus tell the man he would enter Paradise with Him? (Luke 23:43)

_____ Immediately upon dying.

_____ In four days.

_____ After a period of "soul sleep".

_____ Following a time in purgatory.

At least twice before Jesus had raised people from the dead.

What was the name of the ruler of the synagogue whose daughter was raised from the dead? (Mark 5:22-24)

_____

Where did the other resurrection miracle take place? (Luke 7:11-12)

_____

The little child Jesus raised was on her bed at home where she had died. The widow's son was in a coffin being carried to the cemetery.

What was significantly different about the miracle with Lazarus? (John 11:38-39)

_____

_____

What were the words Jesus spoke which brought life to dead Lazarus? (John 11:43)

_____

6. The Effect of the Miracle

Lazarus, although he had come out of the grave, was still not free.

What else was necessary to set him free? (John 11:44)

_____

_____

It is not enough to have life. We need to be free. So many of us have experienced life but have never tasted the freedom of the Holy Spirit. We're still bound in our grave clothes. We need to ask ourselves the question: Am I alive or dead? If I am alive, am I still bound in the old grave wrappings of sin and tradition? Do I need someone to help me, to start the unwinding process? Am I free in the Spirit or still bound in the old bandages of the past? Am I willing to come out of the grave, or do I prefer to remain in the shadows?

What did Jesus say was the purpose of this miracle? (John 11:42)

_____

_____

Jesus said the power to "raise the dead" is available to all believers. However, even Jesus did not bring back to life—or even heal—everyone.

What did Jesus say was the key to His power for miracles? (John 8:28)

_____

_____

A dinner was arranged in Jesus' honor, hosted by Mary, Martha, and Lazarus.

What was Mary's response to Jesus' raising Lazarus? (John 12:1-3)

_____

_____

What did Jesus say was the reason for this spontaneous, loving action? (John 12:7)

_____

_____

What should be our response to this great love that calls us out of darkness into His light? (1 Peter 2:9)

_____

WRAP UP

Jesus gives us a wonderful picture of God. God is not lonely, isolated, passionless. God feels our sorrows, our misery, our anxiety. He weeps with us. He also feels our elation, our joy, our relief—and he laughs with us. The greatest thing Jesus taught us about God is that He is not only a God who can raise the dead, He is a God who cares.

FINAL LESSON

Is this power to "raise the dead" available to all believers? Jesus says it is. Granted, it is seen only rarely—but there have been a number of authenticated instances when God's men and women have heard from God, spoken with authority, and the dead have come back to life.

The secret is hearing from God.

REVIEW QUESTIONS

Circle T (true) or F (false).

1. T   F   When I die, I will be able to live on in heaven if I believe in Jesus.

2. T   F   Like Martha, we all tend to blame God when things go wrong.

3. T   F   Real life exists in the spirit rather than in the body.

4. T   F   What I believe is more important than who I believe in.

5. T   F   Showing emotion is a sign of weakness.

6. T   F   Jesus perfomred the miracle of raising Lazarus from the dead in order to draw attention to Himself.

7. T   F   The secret in raising people from the dead is to hear from God.

8. T   F   Jesus used the help of people in setting Lazarus free.

9. T   F   Telling people about Jesus is the task of all believers.

10. T   F   Even more wonderful than being resurrected from the dead is to receive eternal life.

MEMORY VERSE

John 11:25-26 (Memorize, then write it on these lines.)

_____

_____

_____

_____

_____

_____

NOTES

TRUE OR FALSE ANSWERS:

1-T, 2-T, 3-T, 4-F, 5-F, 6-F, 7-T, 8-T, 9-T, 10-T

93

NOTES

Information on Ordering

For additional copies of this workbook
or
for the Video Tape Series designed
to be used with the workbook . . .
or
for the other titles in
Jamie Buckingham's Holy Land Series
Ten Parables of Jesus
Ten Bible People Like Me
Journey to Spiritual Maturity

write or call:
Paraclete Press
P. O. Box 1568
Orleans, MA 02653
Telephone: 1-800-451-5006
or
buy them at your local Christian bookstore.